Poetic Diversities

Tabitha Edwards-Walton

Energion Publications
Gonzalez, FL
2014

Cover Design: Jody & Henry Neufeld

Cover Image: ID 35466177 © Agsandrew | Dreamstime.com

ISBN10: 1-63199-075-6
ISBN13: 978-1-63199-075-5
Library of Congress Control Number: 2014950187

Energion Publications
P. O. Box 841
Gonzalez, FL 32560

energionpubs.com
pubs@energion.com
850-525-3916

DEDICATION

To my mother
Without her I would not be here today.
She has always provided me with love and support.
And I would have to say she has taught me
to be the woman I am today. I love you, Mom.

And to my number one fan, my son Ray.
He has provided me with so much love and strength
to get through some challenging times
I did not think I could get through.
His drive to live taught me
that if he could do that, then I could do this.
I love you more than life, Ray.
You are my best friend. I love you, son.

ACKNOWLEDGMENTS

A special thank you to Deanna and Ray,
Ashley, Anastasia (Lily), and Astrid,
my parents, Keith and Regina,
Henry and Jody Neufeld at Energion Publications,
Rebeca Enos, Hazel Harper, Debbie Trent,
and God.
Without the love and support of these special people
I would not have been able to do this.
They believed in me and/or inspired me, letting me know
that my words were worth enough to put into a book.

TABLE OF CONTENTS

INTRODUCTION

I started writing poetry over twenty years ago. Back then it was just thoughts I had that I put on paper. I never really imagined anything would come from it. I wrote several poems of feelings I had. I put them away and did not really think much of them again. They were my thoughts, my feelings. I sheltered them. I hid them from the world's eyes.

Occasionally I would share theses thoughts with the people who had inspired me. I found it helped me. It was therapeutic for me to write these poems even if I never shared them with anyone.

Then I went through a period of years where I did not write at all. I found that I missed this part of me. I felt like I had lost something inside of me. It was as if a part of me had vanished.

One day I shared some of my poems again with a couple of close friends and they told me my poems were good. I never believed in myself. I never considered my thoughts on paper were good enough. All I knew was it made me feel good inside.

I knew I had an appreciation for nature. I knew my biggest inspiration was my son so I would write about those things and the writings came more often. I learned that my writings of poetry are filled with pure emotion. They are very heartfelt. I write from the heart.

I have discovered many things about myself along this journey. I have discovered I have an appreciation for the artistic side of life. I love music, art hung in an art gallery, nature, and things others may take for granted because I am in tune with my emotions.

I like to write in first person. I actually like to put myself into the situation even if I have not actually lived it. Some of my poetry is personal and specific to certain individuals in my life. Other poems are my imagination coming to life. I write what feels good at the time. I have no certain style.

Thank you for choosing to read *Poetic Diversities*.

– Tabitha

Poetry is art
through the expression of words
filled with emotions.
The reader determines the beauty
by what one deciphers.

– Tabitha Edwards-Walton

What it Takes to Make A Child Happy

A child needs a lifetime of love and devotions.
It is amazing how a child can grow with these emotions.

A child needs a life time of help and reassurance.
No matter what one may do, give her or him guidance
and confidence.

Be someone that your child can look up to.
Lead them by positive role modeling
because this child will want to be just like you.

Hug, kiss, and tell your child you love them many times a day.
Let your child know she or he is special in her or his own way.

Show your child often that you really do care.
Listen to the stories your child may want to share.

Try to always look your child in the eyes.
Comfort this child when she or he is hurting,
or when she or he cries.

Play with this child as often as you can.
It will not be long before this child is a woman or a man.

Even though there may be many tears along the way.
The smiles and laughter will be there to stay.

HIGH SCHOOL GRADUATION

Today we celebrate and attend your High School Graduation.
Through the years, you built the foundation.

The last milestone of your childhood is soon to be in place;
this brings a new walk of life for you to face.

High School days are soon to be a memory of the past.
For a parent it seems like the time has gone so very fast.

Remember every teacher that you have ever had.
You got through it – so it couldn't have been so bad.

Take with you everything they have taught you,
and apply it to something new.

You will be successful in the things that you do,
Because of the High School years you have been through.

THE LOVE AND BOND BETWEEN MOTHER AND DAUGHTER

Every mom wants to be close to their daughter,
To share moments of love and laughter.
The closeness often begins in the womb;
This is where it is first nourished and starts to bloom.
This bond is usually greater than any other,
This is where they learn to love and need one another.

Most moms hope for happy ever after.
If these bonds don't start before birth they may end in disaster.
There are times when a mom gets to be a mom without giving birth.
This makes that bond more like Heaven here on Earth.

You were born to a man who did not do you right, he is my brother.
And now I am honored to call myself your mother.
That makes our relationship far better than any other.

Sure we have had some ups and downs
but I feel our relationship is closer.
Some biological moms do not share what we have
and for that I would do it all over.
I am so proud to have you as my daughter.
I love you so much.
You make me a very happy mother.
Not only have you made me a mother
but you have also made me a grandmother.
So now you get to share love and laughter with your daughters
and I get to share love and laughter with my beautiful granddaughters.

The Will to Survive

Many times the darkness of Death has knocked on your door.
You would say," Go away! I don't want to see you anymore."
You have determination to survive.
Your strong will makes you strive to stay alive.

This cloak of darkness has often made us stop and pray.
"Please Lord; give us just one more day."
Fragile and frail you would struggle your way through,
because you knew you were not ready to see the heavenly blue.
You had so much purpose, so much love and so much to give;
God answered our prayers and let your live.
You were already stronger than me,
and you were only that of three.

You were a very tiny baby born twelve weeks early.
You weighed just 2.1 lbs. and on a ventilator for two months.
You lived in the NICU for five months,
and you were diagnosed with Lissencephally.
Your life expectancy was projected to be
around two years old with very poor quality.
Today you are doing great.
Walking, talking, and you have an almost normal life.
You are now 10 years old. Thank you Lord!
And thank you Ray, for your strong will to live.
I love you, son.

ADOPTION DAY

Every day that you are alive is a special day.
We get satisfaction to watch you grow and play.

It is our pleasure to hold you, and to love you.
Especially after all the things you have been through.

We are honored to comfort you when you are hurt or sad,
Or to help you during the times that you are upset or mad.

The joys we get when you are happy or when you laugh.
We are so proud we cannot help but to brag on your behalf.

We are here to teach you as well as to learn from you.
You are perfect in our eyes in everything that you do.

The judge granted us the adoption letter.
Our lives changed forever.

We became your parents and you became our son.
Our family became one, the courts said it was all done.

Hand and Hand

Son, please put your hand into mine.
I shall be your strength. Trust in me and you will do just fine.

I will be your balance. I will hold you up when you go to fall.
Just like everything in life, one must start out small.
Together we will start out with small steps.
And one day you shall stride great leaps.

Right now you are unsure of yourself, but I am sure for you.
Take a look back, and reminisce all that you have already been through.

Yes, you have fallen a time or two, but pick yourself up and retry.
And do not get discouraged, fight through the tears. Please do not cry.

Remember the days where you learned to sit and to crawl.
One day you will walk on your own, you are going to do it all.

But until then I hope that you know,
that you can always put your hand in my hand.
Together as long as you need me,
we will walk all over this land.

A Mother's Love

Because I have a mother's love,
I can thank the heavens up above.
Sometimes I don't know the words to say,
but her tenderness and kindness has showed me the way.
The soft touch of my mother's loving hand,
gave me the courage; now on my own I do stand.
Into a woman I did grow;
it is because of a mother's love,
my mother is whom I will forever owe.

This was first written for my mom many years ago. When I first started writing she cried when I gave it to her and I had a plaque made that now hangs on her wall. My writing is more advanced so I will revise this for my mom but the original one has to stay as it is.

A MOTHER'S LOVE II

Every night before I lay down to go to sleep,
I thank the Lord up above;
for giving me a wonderful mother,
that fills me with her endless love.
There are often times that I do not know
the right words to convey.
Mom, I want you to know that your kindness and tenderness
shows me the way.
If I need help, the way you are quick to lend me a gentle hand;
through the years, this has given me courage,
because now on my own I do stand.
Into a woman I did grow.
Mom, it is because I had your wonderful love,
this is what I want you to know.

GOING FROM A WOMAN TO A MOM

Any woman can be a mother,
but it takes a special woman to become a mom.
The most important piece of advice to remember
is to always try and stay calm.

The day I became a mom, I remember saying,
"Do I have what it takes?
Will I be able to love and give this child what he needs?
Will I be able to hold him without getting the shakes?"

I did not want to be just any mom,
I wanted to be best mom I could be.
I knew this little person solely depended upon me.

I wanted to cradle him softly next to my skin.
I wanted to protect him from all the world's evils,
and keep him away from sin.

To be a good mom, I know that I have to allow him
to become independent;
I have to allow him to grow.
The best way to do this is to teach him things
that he needs to know.

I know this is going to be a lifelong process.
I have to teach him things like how to eat, walk, talk,
and how to dress.

I have to continue to teach him things like respect.
As a mom I have to teach him things like cause and effect.

I have to teach him how to do well in schools.
I will have to teach him how to follow society's rules.

I have to show him that I love him every single day.
I also have to try not to smother him
and let him find his own way.

MOMENTS I TREASURED

These were the special moments that I treasured
and that I wanted to keep.
I would lay you down and I would say,
"It is time, my son, to sleep."

You would always ask,
"Why do I have to go night night?
Will you please pull my blankie up?
Will you tuck me in tight?"

You would say, "I want a kiss, a hug" and
"I love you, Mama."
Sometimes you would cry or cause a little drama.

You would laugh, talk and play.
You would just do anything, to get me to stay.

You would want to hold my hand, as you lay in my arms.
You sure knew how – to put on the charms.

Then in the next seconds you drifted into Dream Land.
I would gently rub your hair with the fingers of my hand.
You were asleep for the day.

I would hold you close and just watch you sleep.
I would try not to move, I would not dare make a sound,
not even the slightest peep.
You were lost in peaceful dreams,
and I would kiss your cheek.
I would say, "I love you, Ray."

Sometimes, I would fall asleep too.
There were many nights I would find myself
spending the whole night next to you.

In the morning, when it became a new day,
You would always say, "Mama! The sun is up now! It is time to play!"

ANASTASIA LILLIAN MARTINEZ

The first moment I laid my eyes on you,
oh how you won my heart!
You are beautiful, precious, loving, and smart.
I am your GrandMammy,
and you are my Lily;
I think you are cute, funny and silly.
I never get to talk to you or play with you
or even see you enough;
as a Grandparent this is very rough.
You are the light in my sky after the rains;
you are my rainbow.
You are the very blood in my veins;
and you are the reason that it does flow.
You are my Princess and you forever will be;
I love you so much and thank you
for being all these things to me.

ASTRID ELIZABETH-ROSE MARTINEZ

Precious baby princess bundle,
I love the way you love to cuddle.
Your smile lights my heart like the sun in the sky;
your hugs make me feel special like a beautiful butterfly.
Remember Grand Mammy will always love you.
And I will always be there for you.

LOVE THROUGH ALL YOUR SENSES

Love is the one emotion that should completely devour us
as a human being.

Love through the eyes that allow us to see.
Love though the ears that allows us to hear.
Love through the hands that allow us to feel.
Love through the nose that allows us to smell.
Love through the tongue that allows us to taste.

Go to an Art Gallery where they have the most
colorful paintings hung on the wall.
Take in all the colors, as you look at them for the first time.
Now you are blind!
The beautiful colors are now black!
Go back to the one you love the best,
how many colors can you now recall?
Can you describe the array of colors from the details,
pictured just from your mind?
Listen to your favorite music or song,
with passion that is heartfelt.
Listen to every tone and melody, pay attention to the lyrics,
making sure to hear the different sounds.
Now you are deaf!
Can you still hear the music?
Do you feel the vibrations?
Does it make your heart melt?
Does it still captivate your mood?
Does the music that you are no longer able to hear,
make the pulse of your heart's blood pound?
Embrace the touch of your first born child,
as it is laid in your arms for the first instant.

Feel the moisture, as you wipe away the saline
from your tear-stained eyes when you cry.
Now your hands and arms are gone,
do you still feel the same, or is it different?
The feeling will have to come from your heart,
in the form of love. Go on, give it a try.
Go to a candle shop;
take in all the aromas from the different candle scents.
When they are all mixed together,
the fragrances are very pleasurable to the olfactory nerves.
Now pick out the aroma you like the best.
You can no longer smell. Can you now make out its contents?
Absorb this now with your love.
Did you hold that particular fragrance in your heart's reserves?
Go to a winery with the finest of imported wines.
Taste all the various flavors, all the whites and the reds.
Now your tongue is gone. Find the one you savored as the best.
Thus it is now making your mouth ache and whine.
Not being able to taste these delicious wines
is tearing your heart to shreds.

When you love with all your senses it makes the world more:
Beautiful
Audible
Tangible
Aromatic
Tasteful

THE WEDDING DAY

The groom waits for his beautiful bride at the end of the aisle.
He cannot help but to wear a loving smile.
He takes her hand into his.
They both know this is what happiness is.
Today two people will unify their relationship
as matrimonial friends.
These friends will be with each other
through times of sickness, in health,
and until their time together ends.
Two individuals, with two hearts, and one love, are now about
to show each other just how much they really do care.
For with each other, the rest of their lives,
they are about to share.
Each of them brings with them something
that will make this family a whole.
Now they come before you, one unified soul.

THE MEANING OF HEAVEN
IS DIFFERENT TO EVERYONE

To some Heaven is the biblical place one goes after death.
To others Heaven is when they hear their child
take their first breath.
Some say Heaven is watching the sun rise.
While others may say Heaven is looking into their lover's eyes.

This is what Heaven means to me.
Heaven is what allows me to subsist and to be all that I can be.
Heaven is what allows me to live.
Heaven is what allows me to give.
Heaven is my loving family and my friends.
Heaven is the love that they give me – that never ends.
Heaven is the surroundings that are in the vicinity of me;
that, every day with my own eyes, I am able to see.
My Heaven stretches from the bluest skies,
to the greenest of trees.
Heaven is the softness of all the sands,
and the roar of all the storming seas.

THE JOYS OF CHRISTMAS

The joys that Christmas should bring.
Do people really take time to listen to the angels sing?
It is a time where, because of our sins, a great man had to die.
Nowadays it is about how much one has to buy.
The whole spirit is now lost,
in the endeavor of cost.
No more is it what it used to be.
It is more about "What is it that I should buy thee?"

It is a holiday that has become very rushed.
The whole spirit of Jesus is being crushed.
There are no more stories being told,
only items in a store are being sold.
The greatest present of all is being pushed away.
It was because of Him, that is the reason,
we have this very special day.

The joy of Christmas in my eyes should be;
something that has been given from the heart,
something that is free.
It should not be a time of stress;
but a time that we should all bless.
Christmas has become that of commercial,
and I am sorry, but because of that, I have became impartial.

19

To Find Out Who You Are

To find out who you are,
one does not have to look far.

Take a glimpse inside your heart.
That is the best place to start.

Take the time to listen, and concentrate,
upon what your heart can generate.

This is where I am sure that one will truly hear;
what is really deep inside you,
and that is you are true and sincere.

Do not be so quick to weigh,
what it is that others have to say!

Take time to evaluate yourself as a whole.
This is how you can strengthen your self-control.

JUST HANG ON

When life or situations get us stressed,
sometimes, our emotions allow us to feel depressed.
It is easy to feel the world's weight.
One becomes subdued to this emotional state.

I can only reassure you that I am here for you,
to hold you and love you when you are blue.
My love for you is very true.
So, just hang on and time will get you through.
When life bares too much pressure,
take a deep breath for a refresher.

Again, know that for you I am here,
even when things get severe.
I shall support you with every decision that you shall make,
even if I think they are a mistake.
So just hang on;
and soon your pressures will be gone.

FRIENDSHIP MEMORIES AND TIME

Who knew? A chance pairing of two special boys one May,
would revolve into four people being best friends today?

It all began when they grouped two amazing, wonderful,
      and loving boys together to swim.
This is where and how fabulous friendships started and grew.

The boys connected instantly building a bond.
Each complimented the other.
One would not swim in the deep end.
The other would not put his face in.
As soon as they were paired together, miracles started to begin.
They pushed each other.

This was the best thing that could have ever happened to these two boys.
They became best friends, brothers by another mother.

The story does not end there, as two parents spent time with the boys,
engaging them, they also became the best of friends.

Their friendship started with small talk while the boys swam. They
noticed that the boys were pushing each other
to do things they were not doing prior to the pairing,
They noticed that the boys started showing
how much of themselves they were sharing.

We started doing things outside of swim lessons
that would allow the boys to spend time together.
At first it was staying after, just to let them play.
A pretend walk through a safari
or playing ball in the field, any excuse to stay.

There were birthday parties for the boys,
maybe it was your house or mine,
and often we would just take the boys out to dine.
There were hours in the park,
the circus, the movies, Panama City Beach, bowling, bike riding,
the science museum, and the fireworks in the dark.

Days at the beach with our toes in the sand,
playing in the water, train rides at Wales West,
and of course – Disney World was the best!

It did not matter to us; sometimes we would just go for a walk.
All I do know, the whole time we would just talk.

We have been there for each other during times of despair;
we have helped each other repair.

No matter what kind of mood we are in, we know we can count
on the other to be there. Our advice is always perfect and just
where it is needed. Smiles are always encouraging and warm.
We do not have to judge or try to be someone we are not.
We do not have to lay on the charm because through it all
as long as we have each other, there will not be any harm.

We always let each other know just how much we care;
whether they are good or bad times we have a shoulder or an ear to share.

We have been there for each other during times of illness.
We have been there for times when a marriage was dissolved.
We have been there when a love was found,
and we have been there through the birth of a child.
I know in my heart for two people to go through this together,
a friendship must be solid and sound.

The conversation just flows;
the compassion for each other forever shows.

These friendships will last a lifetime. They will not stop.
Our friendships will only get stronger and create more memories.
They will not end tomorrow or today.
I am thankful each and every day for that special pairing
of two wonderful, amazing, and loving boys, that particular month of May.

DISABILITIES, DIVERSITIES, AND JUDGMENTS

People who feel they have the right to place judgments,
put sadness deep in my heart.
Someone who is diverse, why should they be looked at
differently from the start?

It is such a misfortune to suffer from a disability or disabilities,
whether in the form of learning, mental or physical.
Please talk to them, do not stare at them as if they were aliens,
or place labels upon them that are stereotypical.

When you meet someone who is a different race or if they are gay,
do not disrespect them, do not judge them;
try to find a kind word to say.

Take the time to get to know these people.
It may be an opportunity to learn something new.
After all, it would be boring if everyone was exactly just like you.

Many of them have had to face so many challenges,
that the ordinary person has never had to face thus far.
Yet, these people often are filled with passion
and are very happy to be who they are.

Sure they have struggles in life;
many of their struggles come from people who choose to judge them.
Judging people by appearances, abilities, race, or any other diversity
only causes a world of hurt feelings and mayhem.

HOMELESS

Here we go about our fortunate lives,
as we drive down the busy city street.
Do we really take the time to notice the homeless,
standing on the sidewalks where the roads meet?

Are we too engrossed in our world, to see their faces
or even to get to know their name?
Some could care less, or they may just shake their heads
and say that is a shame.

Very seldom do we wonder
if they have had a bite to eat that day.
We may or may not glance at them,
and then we go on about our merry way.

Rarely does anyone care if they are unprotected from the elements;
the heat, the rain or the cold.
Bet you did not notice what their nationality was,
or if they were young or old?

Did you happen to notice the emotion
that came from the children's eyes, as they did weep?
When they asked their mother,
"Mom, where is it tonight, we will sleep?"

It amazes me how many people are actually mean and cruel.
They really do not care that the shelters are overcrowded and full.
Does it hurt you to offer these homeless people
some spare change or even a buck?
Most of them are people just like you
who are just down on their luck.

IDENTITY LOST

Over the years my identity has been lost.
Now all I know is what I feel the most.
I thought I knew who I was, and who I wanted to be.
At this time, I just want all the emotions,
inside of me, to stop spinning and to be set free.

I am searching inside of my own soul.
I am trying to get out of this whirlwind;
out of this darkened hole.
I know that I am a strong person, but emotionally right now,
I am fragile and at the top of my peak.
I have given so much of my heart
that there is nothing left, because it is so weak.

I know I have created my own madness.
Now I live in my own sadness.
I will continue to reach for the blueness of the sky.
I will hold my head proud and so high.

I know I am a good person
and this emotional whirlwind, will eventually pass on by.
Therefore my identity will again be found,
And once again, I will be me,
a person who is solid and sound.

LIFE IS A PAINFUL SORE

Life is a painful sore,
when you are not able to be with the one that you truly adore.
My heart has been tattered;
my heart has been torn,
from the day my love for you was born.
It is your presence, what I do miss.
I am forever dreaming that it is your lips, that I can kiss.
I stare dreamingly into the endless sky;
it is your name that I do often cry.

When you left you took with you my soul, and a piece of my heart.
Now I am left abandoned because we are so far apart.
How on earth will I ever be able to grow?
There are days I miss you, more than you will ever know.

Life is a painful sore,
when you are not able to be with the one you truly adore.

MANIPULATOR

You think that your cunning ways are smart and
that your actions are discreet.
When the truth is everyone sees the calculated games that you play.
Your sneaky snaked tongue has spoken so many lies that no one
believes a word you now say.

You want to be so powerful and controlling,
so that you look mighty to all.
But your ego is getting the best of you, and oh! –
how the manipulation is turning to make you look ever so small.

The one thing you don't give yourself credit for is you are indeed smart;
However, you lack the compassion in your egotistical heart.
So you have to manipulate situations to make others look bad.
It's hard for me to wrap my head around,
I am sorry you are so lonely, it is really sad.

This is your way of trying to destroy others for self gain.
Why is it that you have to manipulate others like this
and cause them harm or pain?
I know you cannot help these manipulative things that you do.
I actually feel empathy towards you.

To like your misleading ways I will not even pretend.
This I promise you, my integrity I will defend.
In the end I will stand up for my reputation,
I will not surrender to your manipulation,
I will not show defeat.

MY FRIEND CHARD

Chard and I were first introduced at a social event.
We quickly became best of friends;
Chard would go everywhere I went.
All of my friends and family liked Chard
so in the beginning my time with Chard was okay.
Then they verbalized that I would act different when with Chard,
so I started pushing them away.
I felt Chard was good for me, Chard accepted me,
and Chard always listened when I was upset.
Chard would make me feel happy, Chard helped me to cope.
She was becoming my safety net.
Chard and I would spend more and more time alone.
I felt I could spend my time with who I wanted, I was grown.
There were times I could not remember events that we would do.
I would wake up after hours had passed, feeling sick,
and thinking, "What had we been through?"
These moments of not knowing were happening more often than not.
Chard was always right there by my side.
I decided I had to end this friendship to save myself;
it's the only shot I've got.
I went away to a facility that could help me get better without Chard.
Believe me when I say at first, this was very hard.
I will miss my friend Chard,
but I know for my health this is for the best.
I did not want my family and friends to have to lay my body to rest.
My best friend Chard's real name was Chardonnay.
Because I got help in time
I am now able to live another day.

THE ROAD TRAVELED

I traveled a road to nowhere,
I traveled there alone.
The baggage that I brought with me
is what made me take this path.
I had been through a life of hell.
I thought if I left, I could make it on my own.
Little did I know that I would cause
more destruction and my own wrath!
Who am I? I no longer know
because my self-worth ceased to exist.
Others see a person that is glamorous on the outside.
If they could look inside out,
they would see a cyclone of fog and mist.
I see the damage;
there is nothing left, not even my own pride.
I just wanted to escape;
I just wanted to get away.
I did not want to feel;
I just wanted to be numb.
I chose the journey to mind altering substances,
and then I wondered why everything was gray.
I have hit rock bottom.
It was the pain and hurt that I was running from.
For I no longer had feelings about myself or anyone.
I no longer cared.
I did not want to feel any more.

A needle to the arm,
person to person, we often shared.
Inside my mind I felt like I was going to stop
the battle and the war.
I finally found the right road.
I was able to put my horrific baggage behind me.
Never again will I allow my mind to go to overload.
Thank you to the years of therapy
that have helped to set me free.

Man of the House

I grabbed my cars and went outside to play
when the yelling began.
I remember saying to myself,
here we go once again
He who calls himself a man
is no man at all.
He smacked her around
and pushed her into the wall.
One of these days I vowed,
I will show him what it is really like to be a man.
He only does this now because he can.
He does not know the pain I feel inside,
to see and hear my mom cry.
I sat on the front porch as I listened to them fight,
I wished he would die.
He is not my father,
he is just a man, and I am just a child.
The thoughts in my head have gone wild.
The things I could do to end this.
Even though I am small, I had to try.
No more will my mom suffer
no more will she be battered or bruised,
and no more would she cry.
So I got up and walked inside.
I walked over to him and I pushed him aside.
He looked down at me, his eyes filled with hate.

I did not run, I just stood there
like I was Alexander the Great.
I dared him to hit me like he did my mom
but something inside him weakened,
he could not hit a small boy like he battered a woman.
That is the day I knew to him, I became his equal,
I became a man.
He never hit my mom again,
because he knew he would have to go
through the man in the house.
That day to me –
he was as weak as a mouse.

THE GIRL THAT CAME FROM THE TROUBLED HOME

I had a very rough life when I was young,
My parents often spoke to me with a sharp tongue.
They did not show me much attention; I was often neglected.
This left me emotionally hurting and I was deeply affected.
When they decided to show me attention, it was with the power of their hand.
They would smack me around, there were times they would hit me so hard
I was barely able to stand.

I dared not have an exchange negative dialogue,
because if I did I was in a heap of trouble.
Believe me when I say I followed their every command,
because if not – the punishments were double.
I turned my life around when I left their house after high school.
I vowed to never again let anyone neglect me,
abuse me or to make me look like a fool.

I want more from my life then what they could ever give to me.
I want to be independent, I will break the circle,
I will show them, and I will let them see.
I am kind-hearted. I am not like them at all.
There once was a boy who moved into my neighborhood.
Even though we both live in the projects or
low income housing of Beechwood,
I would not let anyone mess with him, I took him under my wing.
As long as I was around, he did not have to worry about anything.

LEAVING ABUSE

The days that were once filled with love are now dark and sad.
Fading fast are the good memories two people once had.
On her own, this woman will try to stand.
She is finally leaving the man
who shows love with the power of his hand.
This is the very man who needs no excuse;
for the emotional and physical abuse.
This man took her to be his wife;
now he only threatens her life.
She is tired of being battered and bruised;
she is always feeling like she is being used.
For her freedom she does now strive;
She is praying to God to stay alive.
Happiness he will not let her find.
He is always trying to manipulate her mind.
His way is obsessive control.
He thinks he owns her mind, body, and soul.
Now that she has found a new love,
he tries to force them to be apart.
This only adds to the pain already deep within her heart.
This woman did walk away.
If you are in a situation such as this, please do not stay.
Find the help that you deserve and that you need.
You are worth it,
save your life because no woman deserves to be hit,
nor do they deserve to bleed.

.

Dear Sweet Angel

I am sorry for all the pain that you had to endure.
Your life was shortened and your death was very traumatic.
I did not know you all that well,
but I held you in my arms, I kissed you good night,
and I told you that every thing would be alright.
I am sorry you suffered at the hands of monsters.
I am thankful that the Lord took you home
where you don't have to suffer any more.
He took you to a place where you can laugh and sing all day.
No more worries for you, sweet angel.
No one will ever hurt you again.
I am sorry so many people let you down.
People that were suppose to love you,
teach you, and to protect you.
Rest in peace, Sweet Angel.
For this poem there is no rhyming pattern because there was no reason.
This little girl was murdered at the hands of monsters.
She was only 3 years old

CONDOLENCE

I give to you my deepest condolence,
to help you through this time of sorrow-filled moments.
The Time has come for your loved one to move along;
they leave behind with you the strength so you can be strong.
I know with this kind of pain and sorrow,
you feel like you do not know if you even want to see tomorrow.

You have to know, that you will always have the memories
that will always last.
The grieving part will soon be of the past.
Do not be sad because you were forced apart.
Remember to always hold their love in your heart.
When it is your time, the joyous day will come,
where your angels will carry you home.
Your loved one will be first in the line to lead the way.
Together in Heaven is where the two of you shall stay.
Together we bow our heads to pray,
as the angels, tenderly escort your loved one away.

"Dear Lord, please be kind to this treasured soul,
as you accept it into your Promise Land.
We know that we will never again hear
the beat of this heart or feel the warmth of this hand.
We also know that this soul is for your taking.
Death is a strong emotional feeling.
So, please help those of us that are left behind,
to get through the grieving and then the healing."

MY SISTER

Stolen from me a sister that I truly do love.
She was taken to a better place, **The Heavens** up above.
I will forever remember her,
but now I can only speak to her through a prayer's whisper.

Every once in a while,
I can see her beautiful smile.
I think of her so often when a rainbow fills the sky.
I question God daily, "Why is it that my sister had to die?"
There was so much pain that was bestowed unto me,
when you took her and made her free.
She was not only my sister, she was my soul mate.
She was taken to Heaven, through the pearl gate.
As the days, months, and the years pass by,
I will never forget her, and sometimes it too makes me want to die.
I know the day will come, where I will see my sister again,
when God calls for me, to come home to heaven's eternal den.

DEAD PERSON'S LAST LIVING HELL

Found by an innocent passerby.
The bones were left where they lie.
This person was traumatized by that of a mad man's hand.
He left the human remains to fossilize into the land.
What stories are to be told?
Will the evidence unfold?
Will these bones convey the horrid tale
of this dead person's last living hell?

Soft Whispers Throughout the Night

Endless thoughts are engulfing my head,
As I lie awake in my bed.
The poems that I do write,
They come from soft whispers throughout the night.

The thoughts are coming alive,
For the right words I do strive.

Soft whispers slowly rise above all.
I stare thoughtfully at the barely lit wall.

THE NIGHT'S RAGE

The thunder is making a barbaric roar;
the lightning is illuminating the night sky.
The rain is pouring down like Niagara Falls.
I realize this is the Angels gathering around to cry.
Yes, they are still with us
and this weeping is their way of letting us know.
Their Angelic tears moisten the Earth
to allow things to grow.
The thunder and lightning is God's way.
God is sending messages to what he wants to convey.
So the next time a storm wakes you in the middle of the night;
Have faith that everything is going to be alright.

Awakened in the Middle of the Night

I was awakened in the middle of the night.
All I heard was the sounds of horrid screaming from fright.
I jumped from my bed yelling, "My God, My God!" My son, was he alright?
I flew up the stairs to my son's room to find him sound asleep in his bed.
A sigh of relief filled my heart and my head.
I remember I mumbled to myself, "hallelujah" that was all I said.
I then realized that I had left the television on
and that is where the screaming was coming from.
I lay back down but unable to sleep now
that my heart was beating like a drum.
I got up and kissed and held him tight.
He is too important to me; I forever want to keep him in my sight.
I tossed and turned for the rest of the night.

NIGHTMARE DISTRACTION

One of Mother Nature's own is calling.
How beautiful the snow is when it is falling.
The moon scantily shines over the blanket of white.
I am lost into the shadows of the darkened night.
The images I am seeing are morbid and unappealing.
Oh, how I need a distraction from this horrid feeling.
I have to get these sinister thoughts out of my head.
I now try to watch the snow as it cascades instead.
I had a nightmare that seemed so real.
Now that I am nervous and scared, that is all that I can feel.
All is quiet while the rest of the world does sleep.
Alone in my solitude, all I can do is weep.
The tears from my eyes no longer fall.
I know now that it was only a nightmare, after all.

Autumn Storm Revised

An autumn storm, off in the distance but close enough for me to hear.
The sound that the soft tender rain brings is drawing near.
The gentle wind glides through the color-changed leaves,
Like that of a breeze.

I am so relaxed; I close my eyes so that I can dream.
The sound of the rain is like that of a running stream.
I cannot think of any other place that I would rather be.
The autumn storm brings relaxation onto me.

Deer Hunter

I go out to the woods before the break of dawn.
I hope to see a buck or even a fawn.
I climb up in my tree stand,
High above the snow-covered land.
The icicles hang from the ends of the tree.
Out here I am a man, I am free.
The air is wintery and still.
I am out here because it is my passion
And I am here at my own will.
I sit patiently, I just look around,
At the snow-covered ground.
I am ever so quiet
So that I do not make any sound.
My heart begins to pulsate and pound.
In the distance, I can see a glimpse of brown;
This is something you would not see in any town.
I make sure to be extra careful, now not to move,
I sit as still as I can.
I verify that it is not that of another man.
The speck of brown casually moves near.
I see that it is indeed, that of a deer.
I draw back my bow and let my arrow go;
This made it worth a day out in the snow.
Now above my fireplaces hangs
The head of a twelve point buck for me to show.

THE BIRDS IN THE MORNING REVISED

Have you ever listened to the sounds of the musical creatures,
throughout the calmness of summer?
They are quite impressive;
they can do their own impression of a classical number.
The crickets can only be heard
as they are hidden out of our vision of sight;
They are masters at camouflaging themselves,
deep within the night.
The chirping of the crickets is what takes us too,
just before the mornings.
They chirp songs of sweet pleasures
and not that of dangerous warnings.
The birds assemble together as they sit inside the trees;
resting upon the branches of the deepest green leaves.
The birds sing their own lovely melodies and synchronized tunes,
that takes us through the summer afternoons.
As the day begins to fade, one may hear a frog or two croak.
They are in the pond, that is next to the hundred year old oak.
They may belch out a jingle,
to let other frogs know that they are available and single.
Once again the time has come for night to fall.
It is wonderful that this musical cycle will start again after all.

What Lies Below the Hues
of the Sun's Glow

I kneel upon the soft white textures of the sand.
I knead the particles with my hand.
I look toward the tranquility of the open sea.
I allow the calmness to absorb into me.

The sun's beams on the ocean, how it makes an astonishing glow.
My mind takes me to an environment just below.
The atmosphere is a breathtaking sight.
The vegetation, the reefs, the corals,
is of greens, yellow, pinks, purples, and white.
There is a kaleidoscope of colors that is forming
right before my eyes.
I am feeling so much emotion,
that it is hard to describe the actual beauty which really applies.

I am in awe at the marine life that passes by.
There are turtles, sea horses, and angel fish in an endless supply.
It is a true mystical world down here.
However, to run out of air is something that I do fear.
I wish I could stay down here forever.
I will always savor my endeavor.
Now the time has come for me to ascend.
As I break through the two planes I see a dolphin friend.
He too is now looking at the sun's hues
beaming through with the radiant glow.
Then he dives to the world I just left below.
Now that I am back upon the white softness of the sand;
I am glad to be on the solid structure of land.

LOST IN CONVERSATION

Walk with me hand in hand,
At the ocean's edge where the water meets the sand,
Taking in the beauty of this, God's created land.
Let us stop for a while, just to listen to the sounds of nature's band.
The sun is shining and bright.
The breeze is warm and light.
The dolphins are at play and the sea gulls are in flight,
Shall we stay here until the sky fades into that of night?

The sun is starting to set.
Please, don't let go of my hand just yet.
I promise these are moments you will not regret!
Nor will you ever want to forget.
The ships are at sea on the horizontal line.
The moon and stars are starting to shine.
The sand is cooling but is still feeling fine.
We are lost in conversation with your hand still in mine.
The peaceful night is starting to turn into another wonderful day.
We did not realize that we had so much to say.
With our hands still entwined we turn and walk away.
The dolphins once again begin to play.

TRIBUTE TO THE FLAG

George Washington first sketched a design for the American Flag out.
He then gave his idea to Betsy Ross, who sewed it out of cloth.
This is how the American Flag came about.

The first Flag was reported to be sewed together by Ross in 1776.
That is how long the Flag has been around.
On the left corner, each of the fifty states is represented
by a white star placed on a blue background.
The first thirteen English colonies, is why the Flag has
thirteen stripes of red and white.
Francis Scott Key came up with the National Anthem;
this speaks about the broad stripes, bright stars and the perilous fight.
Neil Armstrong and Buzz Aldrin left the Flag on the moon,
where they were the first of mankind to take a stand.
Nowadays it can be seen hung from American buildings
and all across the American land.
We have a pledge to the American Flag and it is even given
to the family members of soldiers that have died.
The American Flag is the most recognized symbol for American pride.

Love from the Past

I once had a lover from the past.
However, our love for each other at the time did not last.
We had our reasons,
and decided it was best, if we departed our ways.
I hoped we would not see each other for a while
to avoid the eye contact blaze.

I moved away from that familiar little town.
I often thought of that person,
and wondered what he was doing, and it made me frown.
Did he think of me too?
Does it make him sad and blue?

One day, out of the corner of my eye,
I thought I saw someone that looked just like him pass by.
Was it him? Could it be?
I turned around to see if he was looking back at me.
To my surprise it was him and he was indeed looking back.
I almost fell over from a heart attack.
I ran to him, as he came to me; I was so delighted.
I could feel that he was also excited.
He grabbed my hand and we turned and started to walk.
We found a quiet café, so that we could sit and talk.

The fifteen years that passed; we had so much to say to each other.
I never allowed myself to be happy with another lover.
He told me that he had been married but it did not work,
because he let me slip away, and for that he was such a jerk.
He told me that he had never forgotten me
and had been searching for me.
Never again was he going to set me free.
We are now back together again.
Our love is stronger today
than it was back then.

THE DAY MY CHILD'S PET DIED

The day my child's pet died.
The inconsolable tears he cried.
As a parent it was so tough to watch my child
grieve in this very way.
I held my child close, I tried to comfort him,
but it was hard to find the right words to say.

I knew it was best to tell my child the truth and not to lie.
My child screamed, "I did not get to say good bye!"
I tried to tell him that his pet went to Heaven,
to be with God; our friend would suffer no more.
My child yelled, "God, I need Doc more than you do!"
My child's heart was broken; his pet is what my child ached for.
We had a burial and we placed his pet into the ground;
I hoped my child would then understand,
that his beloved pet was going to the Promised Land.

My child was ever so sad.
And for a long time was even very mad.
I told my child it was okay that these emotions were felt;
that this is how people deal.
It is one of the ways that people are able to heal.
I encouraged my child to pray
or just to talk about the grief.
It really did not matter to me
as long as my child was able to find his relief.

It's Positive!

I had always dreamed of having a baby.
The doctors left me with a glimmer of hope.
They would say, "Well, umm, maybe."
I tried for many years.
The results were always negative which left me in tears.

Finally the doctors told me to face reality;
I must have some sort of abnormality.
I was never going to conceive a child.
This made me depressed and I never smiled.

One day I went to the doctor's office, I was very sick.
The doctor said, "You are pregnant!"
I said, "This must be some kind of sick trick."
I was told I could not EVER have a baby.
He said, "The blood test confirmed it.
It's positive – there is NO maybe."

Once again I left the office in tears.
How could this be possible,
after hearing you cannot get pregnant for so many years?
My eyes were drenched with tears of joy!
Was my baby going to be healthy?
Was it going to be a girl or a boy?

My whole pregnancy I worried and got stressed;
But in the end I truly was blessed.
I gave birth to a beautiful, healthy baby girl.
How this happened – still makes my head spin and whirl.

It Is Not Your Fault He Left

He will always be your father; he is just not ready to be a dad.
You have to know that it is not your fault; try not to let it make you sad.
He is the one making the choice to walk out on you.
It is his preference to leave you behind,
because he has other things to do.

I know your father made you promises he did not keep.
I also know this often makes you want to cry and weep.
Just remember that if I have to, I will be your dad, too.
Together the two of us will be strong and we will get through.

You are still a shining star.
Continue to hold your head high, and be proud of who you are.
He is still your father, even though he is the one who left;
keep him in your heart.
Your love for him will help you
during these times when you are apart.

Maybe one day he will realize that he has made a mistake.
He will see how much he has made your heart break.
There might come a day where he is again ready to be your dad,
So until then – do not hold on to your anger and do not be mad.

THE INTOXICATED DRIVER

The driver of the car was intoxicated.
Years later, I still think about what he did;
I cannot help but to still get frustrated.

That driver took away someone
that was so dear to me.
The driver was incarcerated
and he should not be set free.
The driver should have to think
about the crime he committed.
The justice system worked in my father's favor,
he did not get acquitted.
This does not help with loss that I had to suffer,
because someone chose to drive while impaired.
This person did not have to drink and drive,
if he would have only cared.
I was only a teenager when my father was taken away
by someone who was so self-engrossed.
Did he know that my father was my hero;
he was someone that I needed the most?

I was a daddy's girl. I looked up to my dad
but the driver was not concerned when he took him that day.
That drunken man got behind the wheel of the car,
with impaired judgment and drove that way.
Life had to go on without the presence of my father;
there were times where it was really hard.
I could never again hug him or celebrate his birthday,
not even with a birthday card.
He never got to see me finish school, he never got to see my kids
and this made me want to cry.
This was all because a man drove
while he was drunk and made my father die.

The Poet's Job Search

I felt confident with myself as I walked out the door,
I was dressed to impress.
My fresh printed resume in my attaché case,
I set out to find some success.
I was sure there would be some that would say "no" to a poet
applying to a job, but eventfully someone would say "yes."
I was pretty sure I could persuade a potential employer
and this was not just a guess.

I went into a retail store
where I knew I would not fit in, but I had to try.
I swallowed my pride;
I walked on in holding my head up high.
I introduced myself as a poet looking for a job,
as I described my skills, I looked the manager square in the eye.
The manager said, "There is nothing for you here.
Thank you for stopping by."

The next place I tried that day was a branch of a local bank.
Again I walked in and asked to speak to the manager.
She looked at my resume as if it were blank.
She said, "Please pardon me, but may I be frank?
You lack the skills needed to work here,
there is nothing here for me to even rank."

I walked into a book store;
I asked to speak to the manager on duty.
I asked her if they were hiring.
I told her I was interested in applying,
I said I am organized with my thoughts
and my communication skills were inspiring.
I also let her know that I knew how to paint the words
so that others could understand them with my skills of writing.
Before I left that day she was so impressed.
She offered me the job on the spot;
she was glad that I came inquiring.

THE MYSTICAL GYPSY

The sky was darkening into a graying mist
when Lily-Rose set out with her friend, Alex Twist.
They were going to travel the Earth;
both of them were looking for a new spiritual rebirth.
Their exact destination was unknown.
They knew it was best to stay together
because they could not make it on their own.

They traveled a long time before they got tired
and decided to stop for the night.
Everything was going according to the plan,
everything was feeling just right.
Alex decided it would be fun to drink for a while,
but Lily-Rose got way too tipsy.
This was not good for a pair of traveling gypsies.

She wandered too far away from their camp.
The woods were very dark,
the ground was cold because it was damp.
Lily-Rose called out to Alex but he could not hear her cries.
He was too far away.
She tried to retrace her steps,
but they only made her lose an entire day.
She finally found a cottage, where she stopped to sleep.
She looked inside there was not a soul;
she did not hear a peep.

She cautiously went in,
and that is when the mystical mystery begins.
She sees things floating around the room.
There was a cat flying alone on a broom.
A man calls to her and says,
"Hey would you like to be able to do things like this?
All you have to do is come here
and give me a deep, passionate kiss."
Lily-Rose runs to him because she discovers that it is Alex Twist.
She thought he no longer did exist.
There must have been something in the wine that they drank.
When she finally woke up, her memory of all of this – was blank.

THE RICHEST PEOPLE OF THE BALL

There once was a man and a woman
who were from the same rich town.
These two were not rich at all, in fact they were the poorest,
and everyone was always putting them down.
There was a big masquerade ball,
coming at the end of fall.
People laughed because they knew these two
could not afford the attire to go.
The town folk thought it would be hilarious
if they could get these two individuals to show.
They thought this was a great plan
to further the mockery of the poor.
So several people devised a strategy
to get them there together for sure.

They showed up just as it had been intended,
but to the town's surprise,
this time the mockery was on the town,
because they looked like angels in disguise.
The dance floor came to an abrupt stop
when these two waltzed on by.
The crowd adored them;
it even made a woman start to cry.

The couple continued dance to every song.
They danced all night long.
By the end of the night they were envied by all in the town
because they were the most abundant of all.
They both found the richness of love.
They lived happily ever after.
Yes, this wasn't just a show for the ball.

LOVE THAT IS NO MORE

My identity is slowly fading.
My tears are now cascading.
My body is falling, crawling and trying to stand.
I am begging and pleading for your hand.

Your heart no longer feels the same.
You think this is now a game.
You turn back to see this as a pathetic plea.
You are trying to move on; you want nothing more to do with me.

I am now a mere puddle on the floor.
You are only steps away from actually walking out the door.
You are leaving me, you are walking out of my life.
This pain I am now feeling is cutting me like a knife.

I manage to stumble to my feet, "Baby, without you,
how will I breathe?"
You say, "Know I am doing this because I do still love you,"
as you lie through your teeth.
I cannot turn off my love like it is a light switch.
Without your love, I might as well dig my own ditch.

DEPRESSION

Depression affects many across our country.
For some it is only a small fraction of their lives.
For others it consumes their complete identity.
Depression forces some to leave behind husbands or wives.

It gets too be much for one to bear.
So his or her own life, he or she does take.
Depression then hurts the ones left behind that love and care.
What a tragedy this does make.

Depression got the better of one man today.
This man made everyone laugh for years.
To ease his family's pain, I do pray,
For I know they must be heartbroken and in tears.

Not many could make people laugh like you do!
Your movies and comedy will live forever.
Robin Williams, many will miss you,
But you will continue to give us your laughter.

ALSO FROM ENERGION PUBLICATIONS

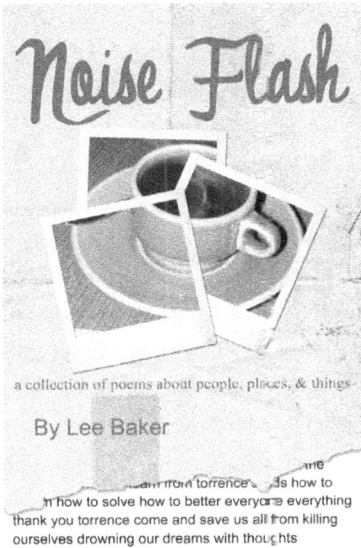

Noise Flash

a collection of poems about people, places, & things

By Lee Baker

...an from torrence. ...ds how to
n how to solve how to better everyone everything
thank you torrence come and save us all from killing
ourselves drowning our dreams with thoughts

"I really enjoyed the process of writing this book and writing is always cheaper than counseling," says Lee Baker. "It's a good outlet for crazy people. In my life, crazy is in abundant supply."

COMING IN 2015 BY TABITHA EDWARDS-WALTON

Poetic Life Experiences

Check Energion.com regularly for updates!

MORE FROM ENERGION PUBLICATIONS

Personal Study

Finding My Way in Christianity	Herold Weiss	$16.99
The Jesus Paradigm	David Alan Black	$17.99
When People Speak for God	Henry Neufeld	$17.99

Christian Living

Faith in the Public Square	Robert D. Cornwall	$16.99
Grief: Finding the Candle of Light	Jody Neufeld	$8.99
Crossing the Street	Robert LaRochelle	$16.99

Bible Study

Learning and Living Scripture	Lentz/Neufeld	$12.99
From Inspiration to Understanding	Edward W. H. Vick	$24.99
Luke: A Participatory Study Guide	Geoffrey Lentz	$8.99
Philippians: A Participatory Study Guide	Bruce Epperly	$9.99
Ephesians: A Participatory Study Guide	Robert D. Cornwall	$9.99
Evidence for the Bible	Elgin Hushbeck, Jr.	

Theology

Creation in Scripture	Herold Weiss	$12.99
Creation: the Christian Doctrine	Edward W. H. Vick	$12.99
Ultimate Allegiance	Robert D. Cornwall	$9.99
History and Christian Faith	Edward W. H. Vick	$9.99
The Church Under the Cross	William Powell Tuck	$11.99
The Journey to the Undiscovered Country	William Powell Tuck	$9.99
Eschatology: A Participatory Study Guide	Edward W. H. Vick	$9.99
Philosophy for Believers	Edward W. H. Vick	$14.99
Christianity and Secularism	Elgin Hushbeck, Jr.	$16.99

Ministry

Clergy Table Talk	Kent Ira Groff	$9.99
So Much Older Then …	Robert LaRochelle	$9.99

Generous Quantity Discounts Available
Dealer Inquiries Welcome
Energion Publications — P.O. Box 841
Gonzalez, FL 32560
Website: http://energionpubs.com
Phone: (850) 525-3916

www.ingramcontent.com/pod-product-compliance
Lightning Source LLC
Chambersburg PA
CBHW022129280326
41933CB00007B/612